MANSA MUSA

Ruler of Ancient Mali

Peggy Pancella

Heinemann Library
Chicago, Illinois

© 2004 Heinemann Library
a division of Reed Elsevier Inc.
Chicago, Illinois

Customer Service 888-454-2279
Visit our website at www.heinemannlibrary.com

Designed by Lisa Buckley
Maps by John Fleck
Photo research by Alan Gottlieb
Printed and Bound in the United States by Lake Book Manufacturing, Inc.

08 07 06 05 04
10 9 8 7 6 5 4 3 2 1

Library of Congress Cataloging-in-Publication Data
Pancella, Peggy
  Mansa Musa / Peggy Pancella.
      p. cm. -- (Historical biographies)
Summary: Presents an overview of Mansa Musa's life as well as his influence on history and the world.
Includes bibliographical references and index.
  ISBN 1-4034-3703-3 (HC) -- ISBN 1-4034-3711-4 (pbk.)
  1. Musa, Sultan of Mali, fl. 1324--Juvenile literature. 2. Mali (Empire)--Kings and rulers--Biography--Juvenile literature. 3. Mali (Empire)--History--Juvenile literature. [1. Musa, Sultan of Mali, fl. 1324. 2. Kings, queens, rulers, etc. 3. Mali (Empire)--History.] I. Title. II. Series.
  DT532.2.M87P36 2003
  966.2'017--dc21
                          2003005921

Acknowledgments
The author and publisher are grateful to the following for permission to reproduce copyright material: Icon, pp. 20, 21, 23 Bibliotheque Nationale de France; p. 5 Franko Khoury/National Museum of African Art/Smithsonian Institution; p. 6 Paul W. Liebhardt/Corbis; pp. 7, 24 Werner Forman/Art Resource; p. 8 Yann Arthaus-Bertrand/ Corbis; pp. 9, 14, 22, 25 Eliot Elisofon Photographic Archives/National Museum of African Art/Smithsonian Institution; p. 10 Bernard and Catherine Desjeux/Corbis; p. 12 Eleanor Clay Ford Fund for African Art/Founders Society Purchase/Detroit Institute for the Arts/78.32; p. 13 Schomburg Center for Research in Black Culture/Astor, Lenox and Tilden Foundations/New York Public Library; p. 15 Art Resource, NY; p. 16 Erich Lessing/Art Resource, NY; p. 17 Kevin Fleming/Corbis; p. 18 Christine Osborne/Corbis; p. 19 Courtesy American Numismatic Society; p. 26 Charles & Josette Lenars/Corbis; p. 27 Franko Khoury/National Museum of African Art/Smithsonian Institution; p. 28 Wolfgang Kaehler/Corbis; p. 29 Curt Carnemark/World Bank Photo Library.

Cover photograph: Bibliotheque Nationale de France

Special thanks to Michelle Rimsa for her comments in preparation of this book.

Some words are shown in bold, **like this.** You can find out what they mean by looking in the glossary.

Many names and terms may be found in the pronunciation guide.

For more information on the image of Mansa Musa that appears on the cover of this book, turn to page 20.

Contents

Who Was Mansa Musa? 4

Growing Up in Mali 6

Daily Life 8

An Unknown Land 10

King of Mali 12

Religious Differences 14

Journeying to Mecca 16

Meeting the Sultan 18

The King Returns 20

Building a Better Mali 22

A Strong Kingdom 24

The Downfall of Mali 26

Mansa Musa's Life 28

Glossary *30*

Time Line *31*

Pronunciation Guide *31*

More Books to Read *31*

Index *32*

Who Was Mansa Musa?

Mansa Musa lived about 700 years ago in western Africa. He ruled a kingdom called Mali for 25 years. Mansa Musa helped Mali grow larger, richer, and stronger.

The world in Mansa Musa's time

In Mansa Musa's day, only a few people traveled to distant lands. They brought things and stories about people from far away. However, western Africa and other large areas were still mostly unknown to the rest of the world.

In the Americas, several native **empires** were growing strong. The Incas, Mayas, and Aztecs built **temples** and roads. They developed calendars and made beautiful artwork.

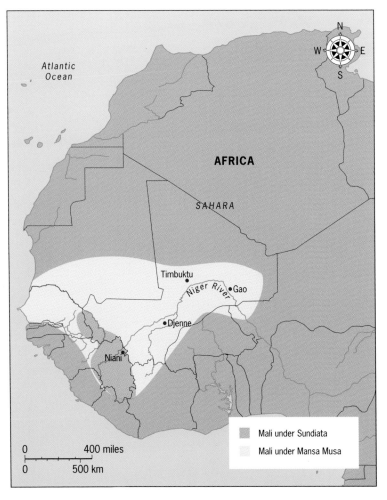

◄ This map shows some of Mali's cities and how far the empire of Mali stretched across Africa.

Atlantic Ocean

AFRICA

SAHARA

Timbuktu

Niger River

Gao

Djenne

Niani

| | Mali under Sundiata |
| | Mali under Mansa Musa |

0   400 miles
0   500 km

In Europe, however, people had been stuck in the same ways of thinking and doing things for many hundreds of years. Diseases were widespread, and many people died.

How do we know about Mansa Musa?

There is not very much information about Mansa Musa and his life. Part of the reason is that records were not written down in Mali when he was alive. Instead, storytellers called **griots** memorized events and retold them later.

There are some writings about Mansa Musa. **Muslim** traders who visited Mali wrote most of them. Some buildings, statues, and artworks also survived. **Archaeologists** have also visited some places in Mali. They have found **artifacts** that give clues about what life was like in Mansa Musa's time.

▶ This figure may have been made to look like one of the soldiers who served the leader Sundiata, who was Mansa Musa's **ancestor.**

Griots

A griot's job is to remember events that happened. A griot uses stories to remind people about the past. In Mansa Musa's time, each **clan** of people had a griot. Kings had their own personal griots. Today, there are still griots in Africa. Sometimes, they play music or sing and dance to help tell their stories.

Key dates

about 1235–1255	Sundiata rules Mali
about 1312	Mansa Musa becomes king of Mali
1324	Mansa Musa makes a **pilgrimage** to Mecca
about 1337	Death of Mansa Musa

Growing Up in Mali

Historians have to guess what Mansa Musa's early life was like. They do know that he was a member of the Keita **clan** and that his **ancestors** included some of Mali's greatest rulers.

Life in a clan

In Mansa Musa's time, many people in western Africa lived in family groups called clans. A clan included parents and children, grandparents, aunts, uncles, and cousins. The oldest man was the clan's leader. The children called one another "brothers" and "sisters" even if they did not have the same parents. They called all the men "father" and all the women "mother."

Young boys and girls stayed home with their mothers. When they turned twelve, they were treated as adults. At that age, most boys learned work skills from the men of the clan. Some boys went to school or learned a craft in the cities. Others joined the army. Girls learned skills for taking care of their homes and families.

◄ **Children were important members of clans in ancient Mali. The children in this present-day photo live in Ségou, a city in Mali.**

Each clan lived in its own small village. The people usually grew food to eat and trade. Most clans also had certain jobs. One clan might be hunters, while another might be weavers.

A family of rulers

Mansa Musa was born into the Keita clan, a family of rulers. His ancestor Sundiata was a powerful leader who built Mali into a strong kingdom. Sundiata's son, Mansa Uli, continued his father's great works.

Historians guess that Mansa Musa was Sundiata's grandson or **grandnephew**. At birth, he was named Kankan Musa. He was not known as Mansa Musa until he came to power later. Mansa is a word that meant "chief," "king," or "emperor."

▲ These are buildings in Kirina, Mali. Kirina was one of three main towns that made up Sundiata's **empire**.

Sundiata

Sundiata was a king's son, but he could not walk or speak. When his father died, Sundiata was too young to rule. His half brother became king instead. Later, Sundiata learned how to walk. His mother took him to another place to keep him safe from his half brother. Sundiata returned to fight a cruel king who had taken over the area. After his brave victory, Sundiata became Mali's leader.

Daily Life

In Mansa Musa's time, most of the people of Mali were very poor. They worked hard, and their lives were simple.

Life in the country

Like young Mansa Musa, most of Mali's people lived with their **clans** in the country. They built small, round homes out of clay. The domed roofs were made of dried grass. People in the countryside usually wore loose-fitting, comfortable clothes.

▼ The wall around this village in Mali protects the people who live there from animals and other dangers.

Most of the people were farmers, growing crops such as cotton, rice, nuts, pumpkins, and watermelons. Clans traded with each other for the foods they needed. Men planted crops, hunted, and made tools and houses. Women wove baskets, made clay pots, and picked the crops. They also cared for the homes and children.

▲ This photo shows a street in Djenné, a city in Mali.

Life in the city

Some city homes were like those in the country. Others were box-shaped with flat wooden roofs. These houses were usually made of bricks. In general, city people were richer and had more belongings than people in the country did.

Just as in the country, people in cities usually wore loose-fitting, comfortable clothes. However, city people wore pants and shirts. Some city workers were teachers, writers, or government **officials.** Others were craftspeople who made tools, clothes, jewelry, and other items. **Blacksmiths** and weavers were especially honored. Malians believed that these workers' skills were gifts from God. The workers were thought to have magical powers that helped them create new products from iron and cloth.

Marriage customs

Malian men could marry as many wives as they wanted, although men who followed the religion of **Islam** could only have up to four wives. A man asked a woman's parents for their permission to marry their daughter. Then he "paid" for his wife by giving her family some sheep or horses. On the wedding day, he gave the bride a gift and welcomed her into his home. Guests would not leave until they received gifts, too!

An Unknown Land

Mansa Musa's **empire** spread across a large area of western Africa. There is still a country called Mali, but its **borders** are different. Mansa Musa's empire included parts of present-day Mali, as well as parts of Mauritania, Guinea, Senegal, Burkina Faso, and other African countries.

▲ Farmers and their cattle are shown in the Sahel region in the photo above.

The Sahel region

The huge Sahara covers much of northern Africa near Mali. Not much can grow or live in this dry, sandy desert area.

South of the Sahara is the Sahel region. This area stretches across Africa, ranging from 125 to 500 miles (200 to 800 kilometers) wide. The Sahel is hot, but most of the area gets about 12 to 35 inches (30 to 90 centimeters) of rain each year.

Several rivers also run through the Sahel. One of these rivers, the Niger, goes through Mali. All this water makes the land a good place to fish, hunt, raise animals, and grow food.

▼ This map shows the routes that traders traveled across Africa.

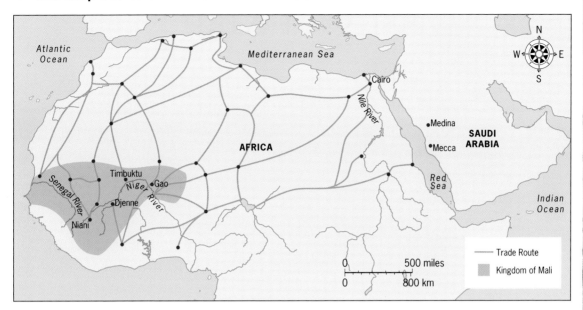

Trade

For a long time, most of the world did not know about Mali and other nearby lands. The giant Sahara was in the way. Then, traders discovered that Mali was rich in gold. They also learned that the Malian people needed salt to **preserve** their food. The Malians were willing to trade their gold for salt.

Soon, traders made trails across the Sahara so they could reach Mali more easily. People also visited Mali's cities. They studied at some of the schools Mansa Musa helped start. The Malian army guarded these trade **routes.** They kept travelers safe from robbers and other dangers.

Blind bartering

Malian gold miners used a secret way of trading called blind **bartering.** The meeting place was not close to the gold mines because the miners did not want anyone to know where their mines were. Traders beat a drum at a meeting place and set down items they wanted to trade. Then they left. Miners put bags of gold dust next to the items, beat the drum, and left. The traders would return and check the amount of gold dust. They could take it and leave, or just go away to show that they wanted more gold.

King of Mali

Mansa Musa's **ancestor** Sundiata ruled Mali for 25 years. Sundiata brought many peoples together in one strong nation. His son, Mansa Uli, was also a powerful ruler. He conquered much land, including several trading centers and many rich goldfields. Mali grew twice as large as the earlier kingdom of Ghana.

However, many rulers who came after Sundiata were not strong leaders. Most of them did not hold power for long. Mali needed a strong ruler to guide the people.

Governing the kingdom

Finally, in about 1312, Mansa Musa took over. **Historians** are not sure of the date because there are so few records from that time. In 1312, Mali had about 40 to 50 million people. They were spread across a large area of land.

Mali was divided into twelve parts, called **provinces.** The leaders of each province answered to Mansa Musa. They controlled some activities in their provinces, but Mansa Musa controlled trade, farming, and other business matters.

▶ **This figure represents a warrior king such as Sundiata. It was made in about the year 1400 in Mali.**

A circle of advisers

A group of **advisers** helped Mansa Musa keep track of what happened in Mali. One **official** handled the **empire's** money. Another made agreements with people from other countries. There were officials in charge of farming, fishing, and working in the forests.

The most important adviser was probably Mansa Musa's **griot.** He had to remember events that happened during Mansa Musa's rule. He also served as the ruler's **spokesman.** The ruler showed his power by not speaking directly to people. Instead, he spoke quietly to his griot. The griot then repeated the message for others to hear.

▲ Griots also ran royal ceremonies, taught the ruler's sons, and led the court's musicians. A present-day griot is shown above. The instrument he is playing is called a *kora.*

Royal life

Mansa Musa led a comfortable life. Many servants helped to run his household. The mansa lived in a beautiful palace decorated with many treasures. His clothes were made of fine cloth and decorated with gold. The mansa met visitors in the palace yard. Musicians played and soldiers stood guard as he climbed onto a special platform. Here, he made laws and handled the empire's business.

Religious Differences

There were two main kinds of religion in Mali. Some people followed the same practices as their **ancestors** had done. Others believed in a religion called **Islam**. People's religious beliefs meant that the two groups sometimes disagreed about what to do and how to do it.

Traditional religion

Older beliefs were most popular among the poor, especially in the countryside. The people believed in one High God who controlled everything. They also believed in good and evil spirits. They wore charms to protect themselves from danger.

Islam

Islam introduced the peaceful teachings of a **prophet** named Mohammed. His followers, called **Muslims**, believe in one God named Allah. Muslims pray regularly and follow certain rules of behavior. They study a holy book called the **Koran**.

Balancing two faiths

Mansa Musa and other African rulers accepted Islam quickly. They hoped to attract more traders—many of whom were Muslims—to their lands.

◀ **People in Mansa Musa's time sang and danced to keep spirits happy. This dancer is shown in a village in Mali in 1959.**

▲ Many Muslim people learned to read and write the Arabic language to study the Koran. This painting shows the holy person Mohammed traveling to heaven.

Islam taught that people were basically equal, no matter where they came from or what their lives were like. This idea helped the different people in Mali get along better.

Mansa Musa and other rulers realized that people might not want to give up their old beliefs. Many rulers tried to please everyone by practicing parts of both religions. For example, Mansa Musa followed most of the rules of Islam. But he also participated in activities that went along with more **traditional** religion. In this way, he hoped to avoid religious disagreements and keep peace in the **empire**.

Mohammed

Mohammed (570–632) was born in Mecca, a city in present-day Saudi Arabia. He believed an angel told him to teach people about God. Mohammed could not read or write, but he told others his message. Mohammed secretly went to the city of Medina, where he continued teaching and gained many followers. By the time Mohammed died, he had brought Islam to much of Arabia.

Journeying to Mecca

As a **Muslim**, Mansa Musa had to follow certain rules. One rule told him to make a **pilgrimage**, or **hajj**, to the holy city of Mecca. Mansa Musa's hajj in 1324 made him very famous.

Planning the journey

Mansa Musa and his workers spent many months preparing for their trip. Mecca was about 3,000 miles (4,800 kilometers) away, so the trip would take a long time. Workers collected horses, camels, cows, and goats. They would ride some of the animals and eat others along the way.

Mansa Musa wanted to show his power by bringing his riches along. One hundred camels each carried about 300 pounds (135 kilograms) of gold. Workers also made 500 walking sticks out of gold.

▲ Mansa Musa and his followers might have looked like this as they were traveling to Mecca.

Setting out

Finally, it was time to begin the journey. Musicians beat royal drums to signal that the hajj was starting. Slaves using the golden staffs led the way. Then came Mansa Musa riding on his own camel. He wore fine silk robes and a **turban** on his head. Royal guards and flag bearers rode nearby.

The crowd going to Mecca was said to have numbered 60,000 people. These included 12,000 of Mansa Musa's own slaves. Inare Kunate, his senior and most important wife, brought along 500 of her maids as well. Other travelers included soldiers, teachers, doctors, **griots**, and **officials** from every **province**.

The **caravan** left Mansa Musa's royal city of Niani. The travelers followed the Niger River to the city of Timbuktu. Then they made their way east across the Sahara.

▼ Mansa Musa and the others with him most likely traveled on camels such as these.

Camels

Camels are well suited to desert travel because the dry heat does not seem to bother them. Camels are able to change fat stored in their bodies to water. Then they do not have to drink for several days. They store energy in a large lump of fat on their backs. Their eyelashes, ears, and noses naturally block out sand, and their eyebrows shade their eyes from the sun.

Meeting the Sultan

After about a year of traveling, Mansa Musa's **caravan** reached Cairo, Egypt. Traders had already brought news of the caravan. The people of Cairo were excited that such a rich and powerful king would come to visit them.

Two great rulers

El Malik en Nasir was the **sultan** of Cairo. He invited Mansa Musa to his palace. El Malik en Nasir welcomed the travelers royally. He held feasts and dances in their honor.

Mansa Musa and his followers stayed with the sultan for several months. When it was time to leave for Mecca, the sultan gave Mansa Musa some gifts of camels, money, food, and supplies.

▶ This photo shows a **mosque** in Cairo, Egypt. Mansa Musa could have visited the mosque when he was in Cairo because it was built in 1304.

Completing the trip

When the caravan reached the holy city of Mecca, Mansa Musa completed his **hajj**. There are no records of his time there, but he probably did the same things most **Muslims** do. They visit a great **mosque** and walk around part of it seven times. They run between two nearby hills and recite certain prayers. They also throw seven stones at three pillars and make an animal **sacrifice**.

Mansa Musa gave money and gifts to the people in both cities to celebrate finishing his hajj. He continued to be generous on the way home. In Cairo, he gave presents of gold to the sultan, the **officials** of the city's court, and other people. Cairo's **merchants** were happy because the travelers spent so much money. The merchants made their prices very high so they could get even more money from the visitors.

▶ Coins like this one were used in Mansa Musa's time.

Money problems

Mansa Musa spent so much and gave so many gifts that he ran out of gold. He had to borrow money to buy supplies for his return trip. The Egyptian lenders knew that the mansa had plenty of riches at home. He could certainly repay them. Therefore, they probably charged Mansa Musa very high **interest.** If the mansa borrowed 300 coins, he would have to pay back about 700 coins!

The King Returns

Mansa Musa's journey was a great success. He made his **hajj** to Mecca and started new trade **routes**. He made friends with rulers, traders, and other people. Mansa Musa also gained better control over his **empire**. His visits and rich gifts made the people want to keep following him.

Newcomers to Mali

Mansa Musa was becoming more interested in **Islam.** He brought several people home with him. He hoped they could help Mali become more of a **Muslim** nation. One newcomer was Abu Ishaq as-Sahili, a builder and poet from Spain. Mansa Musa hoped as-Sahili could improve the way Malian buildings were made.

Mansa Musa also brought four **descendants** of Mohammed, who were known as **sharifs.** The sharifs were honored as important people in Muslim countries. Mansa Musa hoped that Muslim traders might trade more with Mali if some sharifs lived in the area.

▶ This is one of the only drawings that shows what Mansa Musa might have looked like.

Growing fame

As a result of his trip, Mansa Musa became richer and more powerful than ever. He also became more famous. His trip was so grand that many traders and travelers talked and wrote about it. Word spread quickly, even into Europe and parts of Asia.

More and more people were interested in learning about this powerful king. Some of them wanted to visit Mali to meet its ruler and to trade goods. In 1375, a mapmaker named Abraham Cresques drew a map of Africa. It showed Mansa Musa holding out a large gold **nugget** to a trader. Anyone who saw the map could learn about Mansa Musa by reading words on the map.

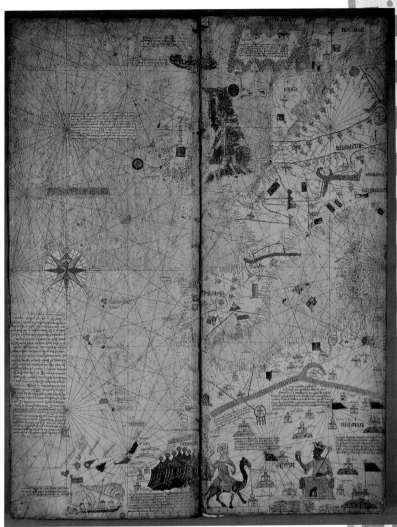

▲ A drawing of Mansa Musa is shown at the bottom right of this map.

Gao

On his return trip, Mansa Musa heard that his **generals** had conquered the city of Gao. This was the capital of Songhay, a neighboring empire. Mansa Musa stopped at Gao and his generals kidnapped two princes. The people of Songhay would not fight him because they were too worried that Mansa Musa might harm the princes.

Building a Better Mali

When Mansa Musa returned to Mali, he was ready to make some changes. He hoped to make Mali grander and stronger than ever before.

A house of prayer

Mansa Musa really wanted to build a **mosque** so Mali's **Muslims** could have a place to pray. He asked Abu Ishaq as-Sahili to design the building.

As-Sahili had trouble finding building materials. Mali had few tall trees or strong stones. As-Sahili made walls of mud bricks with short branches sticking out. The branches helped hold the building together. Workers could climb up on the branches to repair the mud walls. This had to be done every time it rained. In the rainy season, which lasted for several months each year, it was especially hard to keep the building strong.

▲ This mosque was designed by Mansa Musa's builder, Abu Ishaq as-Sahili. It is located in Timbuktu, Mali.

Most Malian buildings were round, with domed grass roofs. However, **Islamic** rules said mosques should be rectangular. As-Sahili figured out how to make a strong building in the right shape. He also used a flat roof. This style became very popular. Many homes and other buildings followed these same patterns.

▲ This drawing shows several different types of houses in Timbuktu.

More buildings

Mansa Musa was very pleased. He asked as-Sahili to design a new palace as well. He also gave money for more mosques, libraries, and other buildings. Many schools were built throughout the **empire**. Most of these buildings were made of mud, but they were cared for so well that some are still standing.

Now there were more places to live, work, study, and pray. Many Malian towns, such as Timbuktu and Djenné, grew into busy cities. With its new buildings, Timbuktu became an important center for culture, education, and trade. Mansa Musa's building projects helped Mali grow in power.

Mosques and prayer

Prayer is very important to Muslims. They pray five times each day. If they can, they go to a mosque at prayer time. This is especially important on Friday, the holy day of the week in Islam. When Muslims cannot get to a mosque, they pray wherever they are. No matter where they are, Muslims always face toward Mecca when they pray.

A Strong Kingdom

Mansa Musa's building projects were not the only changes happening in Mali. Growth in business, laws, education, and other areas made the **empire** stronger.

Trade and business

After Mansa Musa's **hajj**, new trade **routes** connected Mali with more lands than before. Also, more people in other countries had heard of Mansa Musa's rich empire. They sent more traders across the desert.

As trade grew, more kinds of products were bought and sold. These products included copper, cloth, books, and nuts. Farmers, fishers, and animal herders produced enough food to eat and to trade. The kingdom also collected taxes on the goods that were traded.

Protection and laws

Mansa Musa used his large army to guard the trade routes and keep peace within the empire. The soldiers in the army fought off outside attacks and handled smaller problems in the cities and villages. People who committed crimes were brought to court. A judge called a *qadi* decided their punishment.

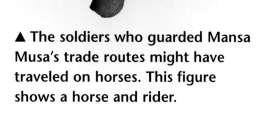

▲ The soldiers who guarded Mansa Musa's trade routes might have traveled on horses. This figure shows a horse and rider.

Education and the arts

Mansa Musa thought education was very important. He made sure his people had places to learn. More and more Malians learned to read and write. Teachers and students from many lands also came to Mali to work and study.

Artists were also valued in Mali. They wove cloth, made clay pots and statues, carved wooden masks, made jewelry, and worked with leather. Musicians, singers, dancers, poets, and storytellers performed all over Mali.

▼ This **mosque** in Timbuktu also serves as a school.

Two kinds of law

Malian courts followed **Islamic** law, but many people still followed **traditional** laws. Islamic law punished only the person who did wrong. Traditional law, however, said the person's whole family or **clan** was responsible. Punishments were different, too. Under Islamic law, a thief's hands were cut off, and some criminals were killed. Traditional law sometimes allowed killing criminals. Usually, though, criminals had to return what they stole and give gifts to their victims.

The Downfall of Mali

Mansa Musa had helped Mali become a great and powerful **empire.** But in about 1337, Mansa Musa died. The kingdom of Mali was never quite the same.

Failing leaders

Mansa Musa's son, Mansa Maghan, became Mali's ruler. Maghan was a weak leader who ruled for only four years. During his rule, warriors attacked Timbuktu many times. They burned its schools and **mosques.** They also destroyed many other buildings.

▲ This is what Timbuktu looks like today. About 20,000 people live there.

Mansa Suleyman ruled next. He helped Mali recover from some of its problems. However, some groups of people quit the empire. They formed their own small states instead.

End of an empire

After Mansa Suleyman's death in about 1360, several weaker leaders tried to take over. The empire grew weak, and its enemies took advantage. Warriors attacked **caravans** and army posts. Outside forces took over some small towns. Also, many more small states simply broke away from the empire.

While Mali was weakening, the eastern kingdom of Songhay was growing stronger. Years earlier, Mansa Musa's **generals** had taken over Songhay's capital, Gao, and kidnapped two princes. After the princes escaped, they returned to Gao and announced that it was no longer part of Mali.

▲ Some of the soldiers who defended Mali might have looked like this horse-and-rider figure. It was made in Mali in the 1300s.

Without Gao, Mali could not trade very well with eastern lands. The empire struggled along for a while, but with only a small part of its former power. By the early 1500s, the empire of Mali had come to an end.

Songhay

The kingdom of Songhay began near the Niger River. Once trade **routes** moved farther east, Songhay started to grow. Even then, it could not fight off Mansa Musa and other powerful enemies. Songhay started to become a strong empire when it regained control of Gao. It grew even larger and stronger than Mali had been. The Songhay empire lasted until 1591.

Mansa Musa's Life

Mansa Musa made Mali into a grand and powerful **empire**. His changes helped Mali become strong. His trade and travels helped people from many places learn about Mali for the first time.

An organized empire

Mansa Musa was a strong leader who tried to make his country a good place to live. His **officials** helped farmers, fishers, and other

▲ This is what the city of Djenné, Mali, looks like today. The city's mosque can be seen in the background.

people work together better. Mansa Musa's army handled problems at home and protected travelers. Mali became known as a safe place where people could get any supplies they needed.

Mansa Musa also brought **Muslim** culture to Mali. He built many **mosques** so the people could pray regularly. Mansa Musa built schools and libraries as well. Finally, he started a court system based on **Islamic** law.

Mali and the world

One of Mansa Musa's most important accomplishments was helping people in other lands learn about Mali. He built friendly relationships with rulers of nearby countries. His travels helped to open new trade **routes**, and his people produced more different kinds of items to trade. Before long, news of the Malian empire spread through Africa and into Europe and Asia.

Very little from Mansa Musa's rule is left today. A few buildings, artworks, and writings are all that survive. But these **artifacts** help to remind people of a great ruler. Mansa Musa brought peace and safety to his part of the world. He expanded trade to build a rich empire in a poor land. He gave many people the chance

▲ This present-day photo shows a group of girls in Mali. Mansa Musa started the first schools in Mali for children like these to attend.

for an education, and he supported a variety of arts. Not only did Mansa Musa improve Mali—he also introduced the rest of the world to a region that had been unknown before.

Glossary

adviser person who gives help or advice

ancestor person from an earlier generation of a family

archaeologist person who finds out about the past by studying the remains of buildings and other objects

artifact object that was made or used by humans in the past

barter to trade goods

blacksmith worker who hammers heated iron to shape it

border edge of a country or an area of land

caravan group of merchants or traders traveling overland together

clan group of relatives

descendant person belonging to a later generation of the same family

empire large land or group of lands ruled by one person or government

general leader in an army

grandnephew son of a person's nephew or niece

griot African historian who remembers and retells stories of past events

hajj pilgrimage to Mecca

historian person who studies and writes about the past

interest extra charge for borrowing money

Islam religion started by the prophet Mohammed

Koran holy book of Islam

merchant person who buys and sells goods for money

mosque building where Muslims worship

Muslim follower of the religion of Islam

nugget lump of a precious metal, such as gold

official person who holds a position in a government or some other organization

pilgrimage journey to a holy place for religious reasons

preserve to make something last or keep it safe

prophet person who delivers a message from a god or predicts future events

province section of a country or empire

route path or way to get somewhere

sacrifice killing of an animal as an offering to the gods

sharif descendant of Mohammed

spokesman person who speaks in place of another

sultan ruler, especially of a Muslim land

temple building in which people worship a god or gods

traditional following the usual pattern of thinking or doing things

turban head covering made of a long cloth wrapped around the head

Time Line

570–632	Life of the **prophet** Mohammed
about 800–1240	Ghana **empire** holds power
about 1235–1255	Sundiata rules in Mali
about 1312	Mansa Musa comes to power
1324	Mansa Musa makes a **pilgrimage** to Mecca
1325	Malian **generals** capture the city of Gao
about 1337	Death of Mansa Musa
about 1360	Death of Mansa Suleyman
1375	Abraham Cresques produces the first known map of western Africa
1464–1591	Songhay empire holds power

Pronunciation Guide

Word	You say
Abu Ishaq as-Sahili	ah-BOO EE-shock ahs-sah-HEE-lee
Gao	GOW
griot	GREE-oh
Keita	KAY-tah
Koran	ko-RAHN
Maghan	MAH-gahn
Mansa Musa	MAHN-suh MOO-suh
mosque	MAHSK
qadi	kah-DEE
Songhay	song-HYE
Suleyman	SOO-lay-mahn
Sundiata	soon-JAH-tuh

More Books to Read

Burns, Khephra. *Mansa Musa: The Lion of Mali.* New York: Harcourt Children's Books, 2001.

Masoff, Joy. *Mali: Land of Gold and Glory.* Waccabuc, N.Y.: Five Ponds Press, 2002.

Shuter, Jane. *Ancient West African Kingdoms.* Chicago: Heinemann Library, 2003.

Wisniewski, David. *Sundiata, Lion King of Mali.* Boston: Houghton Mifflin, 1999.

Index

Allah 14
Arabic 15
archaeologists 5
army 6, 11, 13, 24, 27, 28
art and music 4, 5, 13, 14, 25, 29
as-Sahili, Abu Ishaq 20, 22–23

blind bartering 11
building projects 20, 22–23, 29
Burkina Faso 10

Cairo 18, 19
camels 16, 17, 18
caravans 17, 18, 19, 27
children 6, 8
city life 9, 23
clans 6–7, 8
clothing 8, 9, 13, 16
country life 8, 14
courts 24, 25, 29
Cresques, Abraham 21

Djenné 23

education 6, 15, 23, 25, 29
Egypt 18, 19
en Nasir, el Malik 18

farming 8, 11, 13, 24, 28

Gao 21, 27
Ghana 12
gold 11, 12, 13, 16, 19, 21
government 9, 12, 26, 27
griots 5, 13, 17
Guinea 10

historians 5, 6, 12
homes 6, 8, 9, 22

Inare Kunate 17
Islam 9, 14–15, 22, 23, 25, 29

Keita clan 6, 7
Koran 14, 15

Mali 4, 10–11, 12, 20, 21, 22, 23, 24–29
Mansa Maghan 26
Mansa Musa (Kankan Musa) 4, 5, 11, 15, 25
    ancestors 6, 7, 12
    becomes king 12–13
    clan 6, 7, 8
    death 26
    early life 6–7, 8
    fame 16, 21, 24, 28–29
    family 13, 26, 27
    hajj 16–19, 20
    in Egypt 18, 19
    palace 13, 23
Mansa Suleyman 27
Mansa Uli 7, 12
marriage 9
Mauritania 10
Mecca 15, 16, 19, 23
Medina 15
Mohammed 14, 15, 20
mosques 19, 22, 23, 26, 29
Muslims 5, 14–15, 16, 19, 20, 21, 22, 23, 29

Niger River 11, 17, 27

religion 9, 14–15, 16, 19, 22, 23, 25, 29

Sahara 10, 11, 17
Sahel 10–11
salt 11
schools 6, 11, 23, 25, 29
Senegal 10
sharifs 20
Songhay 21, 27
Sundiata 7, 12

Timbuktu 17, 23, 26
trade 5, 8, 11, 12, 14, 20, 21, 23, 24, 27, 28, 29
trade routes 11, 24, 27, 29

ML   10/03